ACKNOWLEDGEMENTS

I am very pleased to be able to contribute to the Pennfest which is being held at the Quaker Meeting House this year as a celebration of the life and work of William Penn the Quaker. I am not a Quaker - I have been an Anglican until becoming a Bahá'í in recent years - but have long admired William Penn and the Quaker movement, past and present.

I have wanted for many years to put the numerous interesting links between William Penn and Penn Parish into the public domain. The Pennfest has provided the necessary spur to action and it has been a thoroughly enjoyable and rewarding few months.

I couldn't have contemplated the task without my wife's support and her uncomplaining acceptance of my disappearance into the 17th-century for long periods. Central to the enterprise has been the skill and enthusiasm of my long-time colleague Eddie Morton who has, as always, taken on all the complex aspects of the illustrations, photographing, copying, correcting and enhancing the 50-odd images which bring the text so effectively to life. He also designed the front cover.

The librarians in Friends House in London have been as helpful as possible and their American Quaker colleagues in the Friends Historical Library of Swarthmore College and Pennsbury Manor, Morrisville, Pennsylvania have readily supplied several images at no cost. Jean Rollason has made essential, careful and knowledgeable corrections to syntax and punctuation as well as tracking down the source of William Penn's motto, 'Dum clavum teneam'.

Annette Hester of Turville Printing has skilfully and patiently married text and photographs and her husband Stuart and their team have expertly produced the finished article.

I would be pleased to receive any corrections or additions.

Miles Green

FIGURES
(**Bold** indicates colour page)

1 **George Fox**
2 George Fox's visits to Buckinghamshire 1644-71
3 **Admiral Sir William Penn**
4 **The Admiral's purse – front**
5 **The Admiral's purse – back**
6 William Penn, aged 22.
7 Penn-Mead trial plaque
8 Gulielma Springett,
9 William Penn in his later years
10 William Penn's marriage to Hannah Callowhill
11 **William Penn the Squire's four children in c.1662**
12 **William Penn the Squire's family in c.1665**
13 William Penn's bookplate 1703
14 Pennsbury Manor, Morrisville
15 Penn House, Penn Street
16 William Penn the Quaker – his movements 1666-72
17 Holy Trinity, Penn Church in the late 17th-century.
18 Vicar of Penn's letter of 1802 about making the vault
19 1753 nave stone for William Penn's grandson marking the vault below
20 Open entrance to the vault in the north porch in 1987.
21 **The 'Quaker' vault dug in 1753**
22 **Inscribed stone over vault entrance in the north porch**
23 **1766 coffin nameplate for nine year-old Louisa Hannah Penn**
24 Thomas & Lady Juliana Penn
25 Rev. Oscar Muspratt with 1760 coffin nameplate for five year-old William Penn
26 The family of Thomas Penn
27 Letter from a surveyor to Thomas Penn in 1753
28 Family tree of the Penn & Curzon families of Penn Parish
29 Family tree of the 'Quaker' Penn family
30 A rough sketch of the land at the Penn beacon in 1753
31 **William Penn meets Gulielma Springett and Isaac Penington**
32 **Lady Mary Springett**
33 **Hannah Penn**
34 Sketches by the Herald Painter of Admiral Sir William Penn's coat of arms
35 King John's Farm, Chorley Wood
36 Basing House in Rickmansworth
37 Gulielma Penn with handwritten note
38 Letter from Gulielma to William Penn, 16 July 1670
39 **Holy Trinity, Penn Church on 11th Nov 2007**
40 **Penn House, Penn Street**
41 Preface of a pamphlet called Seasonable Caveat against Popery
42 The Baker Diary entry for a fire in the Tyler End Green house in 1698
43 The Rev. Ashley Spencer, Vicar of Tylers Green 1883-1918
44 **The old house in Tyler End Green**
45 **Site of the old house over-looking Tylers Green Common today**
46 Bishop of Pennsylvania window in Penn Church
47 **Jefferys map 1770**
48 Almshouses built in 1831 opposite Penn Church.
49 Glass screen in porch of Penn Church
50 Map of Pennsylvania
51 **Treaty with the Indians, 1682** (inside Back cover)
52 **Jordans Meeting House** (Back cover)

William Penn and Quaker links with Penn Parish

Introduction
The overall aim of this little book is to investigate the links between the parish of Penn and William Penn the Quaker, the founder of Pennsylvania. An opening section on George Fox, the untutored, charismatic founder of Quakerism, and a revered friend and mentor of William Penn, illustrates what it meant to be a Quaker in the second half of the 17th-century. This is followed by a summary of William Penn's life and remarkable achievements. Since mention is made of no fewer than six William Penns, a description is also given of the two others who play an important part in this story - the Admiral who was the Quaker's father; and the Admiral's contemporary, the Lord of the Manor of Penn, designated as William Penn the Squire to avoid confusion.

There are three main themes to the investigation:
- The question of whether or not the Admiral was a descendant of the same family as the Squire has arisen throughout the succeeding centuries. The arguments for and against are considered.
- When William Penn married his first wife, Gulielma Maria Springett, she was living in Tyler End Green in the parish of Penn. The questions of for how long, why and where she was living are carefully examined.
- The story then moves to the 20th-century and the disputes involving two vicars of Penn who were determined advocates of the relationship between the two families and consequently actively encouraged links with the American state of Pennsylvania which was founded by William Penn and named after his father, the Admiral.

George Fox (1624–90)
George Fox, regarded as the founding member of the Quaker[1] movement, came from Leicestershire, the son of a weaver in fairly comfortable circumstances By 1648, he was holding 'great meetings' in the Midlands. He spent his life as a travelling preacher, mostly in England, but he also travelled thousands of miles through newly-settled territory in America where he spent nearly two years (1671-73) and in Holland and Germany. He was imprisoned eight times and endured nearly six years in prison, often in very arduous conditions which many of his followers did not survive. Quakers were routinely ill-treated, but were taught to offer no resistance and he recorded that his own 'body and arms were yellow, black & blue with the bruises received'.

---

[1] George Fox, *The Journal of George Fox,* Norman Penney (ed.), CUP (1911), I, p.395. 'Quakers' was a nickname given to George Fox and his followers as a term of derision by a sharp-witted judge when Fox told him to quake at the name of the Lord

Fox insisted that Christianity should be lived as an everyday way of life; that there was something of the divine spirit in all of us, the 'inward light'; and that everyone could make contact with God without the intermediary of a priest, a set form of service or the performance of rites; that one could wait upon God's guidance in silent worship with any member, man or woman, free to speak if so moved. His freely-expressed view that education at Oxford and Cambridge did not qualify a man to be a minister of Christ and nor did God necessarily dwell in a so-called holy building, made him many enemies. His teaching on passive resistance, scrupulous honesty in every aspect of life, care of the poor, opposition to the death penalty, the freeing of slaves, establishing of schools, and fair wages for servants, set the framework of Quaker belief.

The Quakers represented a strong spiritual reaction against both the unhappy state of the Established Church and the doctrinaire rigidity of the Puritans. They suffered considerable persecution, to some extent even during the Commonwealth years, but particularly after the Restoration when their principled refusal to take an oath of any kind, including one to the king, led to all kinds of difficulties. This was a result of Fox's insistence on observing Christ's injunction in the Sermon on the Mount – "But I say unto you, Swear not at all ….But let your communication be Yea, yea; Nay, nay: for whatsoever is more than these cometh of evil" (Mat. 5, 34-7). Nor would they apply for bail to obtain release from imprisonment.

They also created many unnecessary difficulties for themselves by refusing to comply with the social norms of their day. Gentlemen wore hats even indoors and there was a courtly procedure for greeting others which involved sweeping of the hat and bowing low accompanied by, "Your humble servant, sir". The Quakers opposed such fashionable insincerity and avoided any vanity in dress and flattery in speech. They left their hats on even when talking to the King because their view was that only God deserved such a mark of veneration and they infuriated their elders by addressing them with the familiar form, "thee" and "thou", reserving the formal "you", for God. Thomas Ellwood, a well-known Quaker, recounted how his father, in his effort to prevent him ever appearing covered in his presence, confiscated all his hats and caps and any valuables and money which he could use to buy more.[2] William Penn's second well-known tract dealt with all these matters. It is now known simply as No Cross, No Crown, but the full title was *No Cross, no Crown, or several Sober Reasons Against Hat-Honour, Titular-Respects, You to a single Person, with the*

---

[2] Maria Webb, *The Penns and Peningtons of the Seventeenth Century*, (E. Hicks, Jun., 1891), p 79 onwards

Fig.1 *George Fox,* from an oil painting, now in Swarthmore College, Pennsylvania, once, but no longer, attributed to Peter Lely. It seems unlikely that he or other early Quakers would have sat for their portraits so opposed were they to worldly vanity. This portrait is judged to be 18th-century and so not from life, but it does accord with contemporary descriptions of him as of large build, big-boned, with bright eyes and a piercing gaze. He had long hair hanging in ringlets and needed a hat 'of the largest size'. See discussion of this and other portraits of George Fox and William Penn in John Nickall's, *Some Quaker Portraits Certain and Uncertain*, Friends Historical Society, 1958 (Courtesy of Friends Historical Library of Swarthmore College)

George Fox's visits to Buckinghamshire 1644-71

1644 George Fox first visited Bucks as early as 1644 when he was only 20 years old and was still developing his ideas *[main text, fn.5]*.

1655 By 1655, he had quite a large number of followers in the county, particularly in Chalfont St Peter and High Wycombe *[main text fn.6]*, as well, perhaps, as some of the Penn family from the parish of Penn, since the petition of the Quaker women of Bucks in 1659, which bore 415 signatures, included the signatures of Anne and Elizabeth Penn and the 15 year-old Gulielma Maria Springett. *(see fns 5&6)*

The Journal of George Fox [ed. Norman Penney, CUP (1911)]

George Fox's Journal runs from 1650 to 1675 in two volumes. It was not a daily record of his movements, but was dictated to his son–in-law in 1673-74 whilst they were in prison and supplemented by various letters and papers at Swarthmore Hall in 1675-77. Manuscripts for before 1650 are missing. There are very few specific dates in the Journal.

1656 *Journa*l, I, p.260, 'I went Into Buckingham sheere.. (where Isaac Penington was convinced)…& great meetinges wee had..'
1659 *Journa*l, I, p.334, 'I took boate and went to Kingston & from thence I went to I: Penningtons where I had apointed a meetinge.' *[GF's married daughter lived at Kingston]*
1666 *Journal*, II, p.110, 'I past through Northamptonsheere; & Bedfordshee & Buckkinghamsheere & Oxfordsheere visitinge frends'
1668 *Journal*, II, p.119, 'Into Buckinghamsheere where I had many pretious meetinges'
1669 *Journal*, II, p.154, 'I came Into Oxfordesheere & Buckinghamsheere where I had many pretious meetinges all alonge till I came to London'
1670 *Journal*, II, p. 163, & 'Severall meetinges I had amongst freindes in Midlesex: & in Buckinghamsheere & Oxfordesheere: though in some places there was much threatninge: & frendes much desired mee: for to come to Readinge where most of the frendes was in prison…and so I gave the goaler some sylver… & soe I passed out *[of the prison]*…But the next that came to visitt him hee *[the gaoler]* stoppt to witt Isaace Penningeton and caused him to be made a prisoner.'
[This Journal entry ties in with the letter headed, 'Pen 16 July 1670'; from Gulielma and Mary Pennington to William Penn, in which they report that Isaac Pennington was once more in gaol and that "deare George Fox was heare att two of our meetings and they were very large" (main text fn.53)].
1671 *Journal***,** II, p.176**.** In about August, W.P. and Gulielma together with her mother went with George Fox on a barge down the Thames to Gravesend to see him off on a voyage to America. *[W.P. and Gulielma also went, as a newly-married couple, to meet him at Bristol on his return two years later*

Fig. 2

Apparel and Recreations of the Times....In Defence of the poor despised Quakers, against the Practice and Objections of their Adversaries.[3]

Rather more eccentrically, at George Fox's insistence, they refused to call the days of the week by their accepted names on the grounds that they were named after pagan deities and instead followed the Genesis description of 'first day', 'second day'. Similarly, months were called the first, second and so on. 'Good morning' or 'Good evening' was banned because their use implied that God had made bad days and nights.[4]

George Fox

George Fox first visited Buckinghamshire as early as 1644 when he was only 20 years old and was still developing his ideas. By 1655, he had quite a large number of followers in the county, particularly in Chalfont St Peter and High Wycombe.[5] The petition of the Quaker women of Bucks in 1659 bore 415 signatures including those of the 15 year-old 'Gulielmamaria Springet', William Penn's future wife, her mother Mary Penington, and Anne and Elizabeth Penn, probably sisters of William Penn the Squire.[6]

Admiral Sir William Penn (1621-70)

William Penn the Quaker was the son of Sir William Penn, the leading Admiral of his day, who made his name during the Commonwealth, rising to Rear-Admiral at the age of 23. He was awarded a 12,000 acre estate in Ireland by Cromwell in 1654. He captured Jamaica in 1655, returned too early and was disgraced and briefly imprisoned. He accepted a knighthood from Henry Cromwell in 1658. After the Restoration, he was knighted again by Charles II and was Navy Commissioner from 1660-9, working closely with the Duke of York and Samuel Pepys, the diarist. There are hundreds of references to the Admiral in the Diaries and Pepys liked him on early acquaintance in 1660. 'A very sociable man, and an able man, and very cunning...(we) had a great deal of merry discourse, and find him to be a merry fellow and pretty good natured and sings very bawdy songs... quite uninterested in any puritanical scruples.'[7]

---

[3] William Penn, *No Cross, No Crown*, William Sessions Book Trust, The Ebor Press, York, England, (1981), p.x
[4] Vernon Noble, *George Fox*, Friends Home Service Committee, London (1969), provided almost all the material for the summary above
[5] *Victoria County History*, Bucks, Vol 1 (1925), p 331
[6] Friends House Library, London, Tract, Box 52/13. It was a printed petition to Parliament by over 7,000 'handmaids & daughters of the Lord, and such as feels the oppression of Tithes', listed under their counties
[7] Henry B.Wheatley, *The Diary of Samuel Pepys*, George Bell & Sons, London, (1897), I, pp.238, 257

Fig. 3 *Admiral Sir William Penn* by Peter Lely, shown wearing his dress sword and coat. (Copyright National Maritime Museum, Greenwich, London)

Figs. 4&5 *The Admiral's purse* when sold at Christie's, South Kensington for £50,000 in 1987 to a U.S. museum The brightly coloured silks of this 17th-century needlework show the Admiral with his dog Port on the front; and on the back there are the Bucks Penn family arms 'differenced' with a crescent to show he was from a cadet line - as he believed himself to be.   Port presumably commemorates Penn's capture of Port Royal, Jamaica, in 1655 (Christie's)

But soon he had hardly a good word to say for him, probably resenting his superior knowledge and intimacy with the Duke of York, the King's brother, who was in charge of the Navy.

William Penn the Quaker (1644-1718)

As the only son of the distinguished Admiral who had been Captain of the Fleet under the Duke of York in the recent successful war against the Dutch, William Penn had great prospects: he had entrée to the Court through his father's friendship with the Duke of York, he had family estates in Ireland, was educated at Christ Church, Oxford, had studied law at Lincoln's Inn, and was possessed of charm, athleticism and good looks. But his association with a troublesome sect brought ridicule. Its members, led by a ranting fellow called George Fox, were thought by some to be Jesuits in disguise, and thousands of them were in prison. All this caused great distress to the Admiral, of whom the young Quaker was very fond, looking upon him as 'both a father and a friend'. William was also devoted to his Dutch mother, whom Samuel Pepys considered to have more wit than her husband. Nevertheless, William was implacable in his Quaker allegiance and later spoke of 'divine impressions' he had experienced between the ages of 11 and 15.

Fig. 6 *William Penn,* aged 22. The original was supposedly painted in Dublin in 1666, but has a very uncertain provenance. This is a copy painted in 1909 (Christ Church, Oxford)

This is what John Aubrey, the contemporary antiquary, wrote about him:
'He very early delighted in retirement; much given to reading and meditating of the Scriptures, and at 14 had marked over the Bible. Oftentimes at 13 or 14 in his meditations ravisht with joy, and dissolved into teares. The first Sense he had of God was when he was 11 yeares old at Chigwell, being retired in a chamber alone; he was so suddenly surprised with an inward comfort and (as he thought) an externall glory in the roome that he has many times sayd that from thence he had the Seale of divinity and Immortality, that there was a God and that the Soule of man was capable of enjoying his divine communications.'[8]

---

[8] John Aubrey, *Brief Lives,* ed. Anthony Powell, London (1949), p.360. William Penn gave Aubrey (1626-97), unasked, 600 acres in Pennsylvania and advised him to plant it with French Protestants

William was expelled from Oxford for refusing to wear the college cap and gown; for discussing the absurdities of religious persecution with his fellow students and for asserting the scriptural truth of Quaker doctrines. His father sent him off for a two-year tour of the continent, then to Lincoln's Inn and finally to manage the family estates in Ireland, to try to cure him of his absurd ideas, but to no avail. Pepys recorded in his diary on 29 December 1667 that 'Mr Will Pen, who is lately come over from Ireland, is a Quaker again, or some very melancholy thing; that he cares for no company, nor comes into any – which is a pleasant thing, after his being abroad so long – and his father such a hypocritical rogue, and at this time an Atheist'.[9] Penn had been sent to prison in Ireland and now refused to take off his hat when summoned to see his father. He was forbidden the house and for nearly two years was dependent on help from his Quaker friends and his mother for sustenance.

For the most part, Fox's followers were from the 'lower orders': tradesman, craftsmen, and farming folk, with a smattering of teachers, soldiers and some substantial yeomen. William Penn therefore stood out and in his mid-twenties began to write controversial tracts against orthodox belief for which he was soon imprisoned in the Tower for blasphemy.[10] Pepys was 'mightily' impressed with William Penn's first such book 'against the Trinity'… 'I got my wife to read it to me, and I find it so well writ, as I think it too good for him ever to have writ it – and it is a serious book and not fit for everybody to read. And so to supper and bed'.[11] It was while he was in prison on this occasion that he wrote the first version of *No Cross, No Crown* (see p.4 above).

In the late summer of 1670, he and William Mead(e), a prosperous linen-draper and a recent convert to Quakerism who later married George Fox's step-daughter, were at the centre of a cause célèbre when they were charged at the Old Bailey with causing a riot after he had addressed a public gathering outside a Quaker meeting house which had been forcibly closed by soldiers. The jury continually refused to find Penn guilty as charged, despite threats that their throats would be cut and their noses slit and despite being locked up without food or drink. Four times they refused and were locked up for yet another night, but still they refused and were fined and imprisoned. They refused to pay their fines, but were eventually released. The trial aroused tremendous public interest

---

[9] Henry B.Wheatley, *op. cit.*, VII, p.253
[10] Mary Maples Dunn & Richard S.Dunn (eds.), *The Papers of William Penn*, University of Pennsylvania Press (1981), Vol 1, p.86 n.4. George Fox wrote on 25 May 1677 that WP's hair 'shed away' during this imprisonment
[11] Henry B.Wheatley, *op. cit.,* VIII, p.227. The book which so impressed Pepys was *The Sandy Foundation Shaken*

> **Near this Site**
> **WILLIAM PENN and WILLIAM MEAD**
> were tried in 1670
> for preaching to an unlawful assembly
> in Grace Church Street
> This tablet Commemorates
> The courage and endurance of the Jury Thos Vere, Edward Bushell
> and ten others who refused to give a Verdict against them, although
> locked up without food for two nights, and were fined for their final
> Verdict of Not Guilty
> The case of these Jurymen was reviewed on a Writ of Habeas Corpus
> and Chief Justice Vaughan delivered the opinion of the Court
> which established "The Right of Juries" to give their Verdict
> according to their Convictions

Fig. 7 *Penn-Mead trial.* A large marble plaque commemorating the famous trial has been placed in the original entrance lobby of the Central Criminal Court on the site of Newgate prison which was adjacent to where the trial was held (Library of the Society of Friends, London)

and established the right of a jury to return a verdict according to its conscience. Penn was regarded as a champion of justice.

His liberty was purchased because his father was very ill and wanted to see his son. The Admiral died a week later at the age of only 49 very much reconciled to his son's beliefs. A contemporary diarist observed, 'But which is most remarkable, he that opposed his sonne's way…did himselfe embrace this faith, recommending to his son, the plainesse and self deniall of it, sayeing Keep to the plainesse of your way and you will make an end of the priests to the end of the earth. And so he deceased, desiring that none but his son William should close his eies (which he did).'[12]

Five months later, William Penn was back in Newgate prison, 'a stinking jail' as he described it, for six months. He was released in August 1671 and joined Gulielma Springett, the step-daughter of Isaac Pennington, and her mother to see off George Fox and his band of missionaries on their voyage to America. Next

---

[12] John Aubrey, *Brief Lives*, ed. Anthony Powell, London (1949), p.362

Fig. 8 *Gulielma Springett,* William Penn's first wife. Uncertain provenance (Frontispiece, Maria Webb's *Penns and Peningtons*)

he made his first missionary visit to the Netherlands and some of the German states before returning in late October to spend a month in East Anglia helping Quakers there. He returned via London to Buckinghamshire, probably in early December. He and Gulielma declared their intention of marriage to their Quaker Meeting in February and were married in April 1672.[13]

He continued to write and preach and in 1673 he used his friendship with the Duke of York to have George Fox released from jail. He then turned his attention to America, from where George Fox had recently returned, and drew up a constitution for a new colony of West New Jersey remarkable for its democratic provisions and for its guarantee of freedom of worship. Many Quakers took advantage of it. This put an even more ambitious idea into his head, which he called his 'holy experiment', of establishing a colony alongside New Jersey where Quaker ideals could be put into practice. The Crown had owed his father about £16,000 and in discharge of this he asked for land on the western bank of the Delaware river. The King agreed and in 1681 made him absolute proprietor of a vast and fertile province almost the size of England. William Penn's first proposal that it should be called New Wales was rejected because the King's secretary, a Welshman, objected.[14] His second suggestion was Sylvania and the King accepted this, but only if prefixed by 'Penn' as a tribute to the Admiral. So Pennsylvania it was, despite Penn's concern 'lest it should be looked on as a vanity in me' (see map at Fig.50). The following year the Duke of York added the tiny adjacent province of what is now the state of Delaware.[15]

The constitution he framed for the province was far ahead of its time, including liberal and humane principles such as: democratic government by election; absolute freedom of worship; all trials by jury; the death penalty for wilful murder only; prisons to be places of work and reformation, with reparation from a felon's estate where possible, and children to be taught a trade from the age of

---

[13] Edwin B.Bonner & David Fraser (eds.), *The Papers of William Penn*, University of Pennsylvania (1996), Vol 5, p. 133, 137, outline W.P.'s movements in the seven months leading up to his marriage
[14] Maria Webb, *The Penns and Peningtons of the 17th-century,* (E.Hicks Jun. 1891), p.260.
[15] Pennsylvania is 46,055 sq miles, and Delaware 2,490 sq miles, which makes them 96.5% of England's 50,352 sq miles

twelve. In 1682, he made the eight-week voyage to America on board the Welcome accompanied by about a 60 emigrants, mostly Quakers. He played an active part in the planning of Philadelphia on the Delaware River and established excellent relations with the Indians making it clear that he regarded them as 'neighbours and friends under the same God' and insisting that settlers acquire land by purchase and not by force (see Fig. 50). He gave George Fox more than 1,000 acres.[16] Delaware was included under the same Governor. He stayed for only two years and was not able to return again until 1699 when he stayed for another two years. This time he built himself a mansion by the Delaware, which he called Pennsbury, planted with trees sent out from England.

After George Fox's death in 1691, William Penn was generally regarded as his successor. He was a man of great wisdom as particularly evidenced by this quotation from *Some Fruits of Solitude* written in 1693 – 'The humble, meek, merciful, just, pious, and devout souls are everywhere of one religion; and when death has taken off the mask they will know one another, though the divers liveries they wear here make them strangers'.

Fig. 9 *William Penn* depicted on a medallion based on his most authentic known image, a bust made shortly after his death by Silvanus Bevan, a London Quaker, who had known him (Copied from Maria Webb's Penns and Peningtons)

Fig. 10 *William Penn's marriage to Hannah Callowhill.* They were married in the Friends Meeting House in Bristol on March 5, 1696. The painting is by Ernest Board (1877-1934) who went to school in Bristol. It was exhibited at Bristol Art Gallery in 1925 and may have been painted then. (From a photograph at the Library of the Society of Friends, London)

Gulielma died in 1694 and he married again two years later to Hannah Callowhill, 28 years younger, from a prosperous Bristol Quaker family. They had seven children (see Fig.29). She was acting Proprietor from 1712 after her husband suffered a series of strokes, until her death in 1726. He died in 1718 and was buried in the grounds of Jordans meeting house where he used to worship.[17]

---

[16] George Fox, *Journal*, Norman Penney (ed.), CUP (1911), Vol II, p.354.
[17] Vernon Noble, *William Penn*, Friends Home Service Committee, London (1971) provided much of the material for this summary.

William Penn the Squire (1628-93)
The third William Penn central to this story was the Lord of the Manor of Penn, the owner of a large part of the parish and the latest representative of a family line which stretched back to the earliest surviving records of the 12th-century. 'The Penns, Hampdens & Tyrringhams are commonly esteemed the oldest Familys in Bucks', observed a near-contemporary Vicar.[18] He was one of five brothers and five sisters and inherited at the age of 13. Like most Buckinghamshire gentry he seems to have sympathised with the Commonwealth since he was Sheriff of the county in 1656 at the age of 28, but he wisely headed the county's subscription list for Charles II's restoration in 1660. He was the father of Roger Penn, who was to be the last of his family's name, and of Sarah who married Nathaniel Curzon, the direct forebear of the Earls Howe. (See Fig.29)

Evidence for a family link
The question which has intrigued many succeeding generations up to the present day is whether or not the Admiral and his descendants were related to the Penns of Penn Parish. Evidence suggesting that this could be the case is provided by numerous well-established facts.

Relation of kindred was always acknowledged. Granville Penn (1761-1844), a grandson of William Penn the Quaker, wrote that 'Relation of kindred was always mutually claimed and acknowledged between the family of Sir William Penn and the Penns of Penn in Bucks, now represented by Earl Howe…'[19]

The memorial tablet to Admiral Sir William Penn in the church of St Mary Redcliffe in Bristol, where he had been born and where he was buried close to his mother in 1670 , says '... of the Penns of Penn Lodge in the County of Wilts, and those Penns of Penn in the County of Bucks'.[20]

The use of the same family arms as the Penns of Penn. The arms appear in many places, for instance: on the Admiral's monument in the church of St Mary Redcliffe, Bristol,[21] and on his silk purse recently sold by Christie's the auctioneers;[22] (see Figs.4&5) on the seal of Pennsylvania province while the

---

[18] Rev. Benjamin Robertshaw, Vicar of Penn 1716-28. His Memoirs are held in the Bucks Archaeological Society's library at Aylesbury, MISC/Box 1/32/56
[19] Granville Penn, *Memorials of the professional life and times of Sir William Penn, Knt*, London (1833), II, p.575
[20] Brigadier O.F.G. Hogg, *Further light on the ancestry of William Penn*, The Society of Genealogists (1964), pp.33, 39
[21] Brigadier O.F.G. Hogg, *op. cit.*, facing p.32, pp.34-36
[22] Christie's of South Kensington, London, Rostrum, June-July 1987

Fig. 11 *William Penn the Squire's four children* in c.1662 by F.van Hees. His son, John, carrying the small hawk, is still in skirts. His eldest daughter Elizabeth is nearest the dog. Next to her is Sarah, the second daughter, who was to marry Nathaniel Curzon. The present Earl Howe is their descendant. (Eddie Morton, courtesy of Earl Howe)

Fig. 12 *William Penn the Squire's family* in c.1665 by F.van Hees. The four angels at the top corner represent young children who have died. There were at least 10 children, but only Sarah married (Eddie Morton, courtesy of Earl Howe)

Penn family was its Proprietor; and on the engraving of Benjamin West's 1682 Treaty painting in Penn House.

In the safe in the vestry of Penn church there is a leather-bound 1668 hymn book with the name Nicolas Sprague, dated March 6th 1669, written on the flyleaf. Unexpectedly, it has William Penn the Quaker's book plate, dated 1703, pasted on to the inside of the front cover. It was a surprise to find that he sang hymns. The book plate shows that he was using the local Penn arms without the 'differencing' with a crescent used by his father. It also shows that he had adopted a motto, *Dum clavum teneam,* which can be translated as 'provided that I hold the tiller', an appropriate sentiment for his role as the Proprietor of Pennsylvania and Delaware.23

Fig. 13 *William Penn's bookplate* in the vestry safe in Holy Trinity Church, Penn

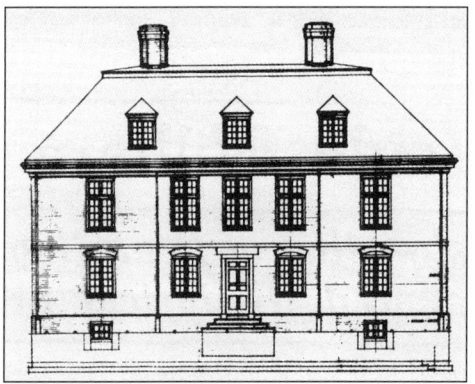

Fig. 14 *Pennsbury Manor,* Morrisville, Pennsylvania. William Penn built the original house in the 1690s, but it was in ruins by 1800. It was rebuilt in 1937 (Pennsbury Manor)

Pennsbury Manor, the name of William Penn the Quaker's house in Pennsylvania was presumably named after the Penn family's original manor house at what is now Penbury Farm, not far from Penn Church.

Visit to Penn House. William Penn the Quaker's Irish Journal records a visit to Penn Street with Gulielma

---

23 The Vicar of Penn refers to the hymn book in a record made in 1962 and there was a note with it saying it had been bought in a Book Fair. The motto comes from Virgil's Aeneid V, 177. The full quote is 'dum clavum rectum teneam', with 'rectum' adding the meaning of 'steady' and is used in the context of holding the ship of state steady in stormy weather. Virgil may well have been borrowing from Cicero who wrote on similar themes. This is apparently now registered as WP's motto in the USA. A website entry claims that there is a similar bookplate in a bible in the Historical Society of Pennsylvania and there is another one, also dated 1703, in Friends House, London. After his return from his second stay in Pennsylvania WP must have been getting his library in order

Fig. 15
Penn House, Penn Street (Eddie Morton)

Springett on 18 Sep 1669, two and a half years before they got married. [24] Penn House, the seat of William Penn the Squire, is in Penn Street and was the only house there of any significance (see map at Fig.47). We know from the Quaker's own account that 'A sister of the family of Penn in Buckinghamshire, a young woman delighting in the finery and pleasures of the world, was seized with a violent illness that proved mortal to her.' She had a vision of Christ 'in the likeness of a plain countryman without any trimming or ornament whatever; and that his servants ought to be like Him'. She said to those around her, "Bring me my new clothes, take off the lace and finery"; and charged her relations not to deck and adorn themselves after the manner of the world. [25]

We saw earlier that the petition of the Quaker women of Bucks, in 1659, bore 415 signatures. They included those of Anne and Elizabeth Penn. The Parish register shows that William Penn, the Squire had a sister Elizabeth, a year older than him and records the burial of 'Mrs Elizabeth Penn' on 7 Jan 1670 (i.e. 1671 new style), and of a younger sister, Mrs Susan Penn, a week earlier.[26] The death of these two sisters only a week apart indicates a 'violent illness'. If Elizabeth was the 1659 signatory she was aged 43 when she died and was already a Quaker, but Susan, who would have been 34, is the likely Quaker heroine of the

---

[24] William Penn, *My Irish Journal*, 1669-1670, Isabel Grubb (ed.), Longmans, Green and Co (1952), p.18

[25] William Penn, *No Cross, No Crown*, William Sessions Book Trust, The Ebor Press, York, England, (1981), pp.viii – xiii, 444-5. William C. Braithwaite, *The Second period of Quakerism*, MacMillan (1921), p.61, n.6, explains that William Penn wrote his first essay to bear the title *No Cross, No Crown* during an imprisonment of seven months in The Tower of London in 1668 and it was published as a pamphlet of 111 pages in 1669, but it was effectively completely rewritten in 1682 with nearly 600 pages and a greatly enlarged number of testimonies. Both original editions were inspected in the Friends House Library and this particular testimony is not in the 1668 version, but is in that of 1682, as is a testimony from Admiral Penn.

[26] *Penn Parish Register* shows that the William Penn, the Squire, born in 1628, had a sister Elizabeth born a year earlier. We know from the memorial brass in Penn Church, he was one of 5 sons and 5 daughters and the Parish Register shows a sister Susanna, born on 28 Sep 1635, but no Anne. It seems reasonable to assume that Susanna and Susan were the same person. Mrs stood for Mistress and did not necessarily indicate a married woman.

William Penn the Quaker - his movements 1666-72

1666-67 In Ireland
1667-68 In England. Met Gulielma Springett

1669
Jan-Sep WP in prison in the Tower of London for 8 months - for writing against the Holy Trinity.
　　　　Wrote first version of *No Cross, No Crown in prison*. Father sent him to Ireland

15 Sep	Departed from London	}
16 Sep	I came to Isaac Penington's	}
17 Sep	I left Amersham, but at Maidenhead missing of my servant	}
	I returned to Isaac Penington's	}
18 Sep	I went with Guli Springett to **Penn Street**; returned at night	} *My Irish*
19 Sep	Guli Springett, Sarah Hersent, etc went on foot to meeting	} *Journal*
	at Russell's and I with them	} *1669-1670*
20 Sep	Isaac Penington, John Penington, Mary Penington, John Giggour	} by
	and myself went for Reading. Guli Springett and Thomas Ellwood	} William Penn
	accompanied us beyond Maidenhead.	}
	We arrived at Reading, visited the prisoners	}
22 Sep	We met that night at Bristol	}
26 Sep	We came to Cork (Ireland)	}

1670
16 Jul　Letter, headed 'Pen', from Guli Springett and her mother Mary Penington to W.P. (who was still
　　　　in Ireland), reporting that Isaac Penington was once more in gaol and that 'deare George Fox was
　　　　heare att two of our meetings and they were very large'
Aug　　W.P. left Ireland (*My Irish Journal*, p.17)
14 Aug　WP arrested in London for speaking at an open Quaker meeting.
1-5 Sep　Famous Penn-Mead(e) trial at Old Bailey, when jury refused to find them guilty of causing a riot.
15 Sep　Father, Admiral Sir William Penn dies only a week after his son's release purchased.
30 Dec　Mrs Susan Penn, the youngest of William Penn the Squire's five sisters, is buried at Penn Church
　　　　(age 34).

1671
7 Jan　　Mrs Eliz. Penn, elder sister of William Penn the Squire, buried at Penn Church (age 43).
　　　　In a 1682 edition of *No Cross, No Crown*), W.P. told of a sister of the family of **Penn** in
　　　　Buckinghamshire who became a Quaker on her deathbed.
23 Jan　Preface to the 2nd Edition of a pamphlet called *Seasonable Caveat against Popery*, printed in
　　　　London, has 'W.**P. Penn,** Buckinghamshire, the 23rd of the 11th Moneth 1670' (ie 23 Jan 1671,
　　　　new style)
5 Feb　WP Started 6 months imprisonment in Newgate prison.
24 May　Letter from George Fox to W.P. addressed 'att **Tilleringreen**'. (W.P. was still in Newgate prison
　　　　and apparently the letter was to be forwarded to him by Guli Springett)
Aug　　George Fox was sailing to America and WP, Gulielma & her mother went down by barge to
　　　　below Gravesend to see him off. (They all went Bristol two years later to welcome him back).
Oct?　　Marriage settlement between WP and Gulielma Springett.

1672
7 Feb　　The Monthly Meeting Book records the first declaration of the intention of marriage between
　　　　"William Penn of Walthamstow in the county of Essex and Gulielma Maria Springett of **Tiler
　　　　End Green** in the parish of Penn in the County of Bucks." 'Consent and approbation' was given
　　　　at the following Meeting on 6 March 1672.
4 April　The marriage took place at King's Farm, Chorley Wood and Gulielma was recorded as of **Penn**.
　　　　They went to live at Basing House in Rickmansworth for five years.

Fig. 16

Quaker's story.[27]   William Penn was in Penn two weeks after the funerals (see Fig.16 opposite).   He would at least have had a first-hand account from the family. He may well have visited the sick ladies whom he and they believed to be cousins and who would anyway have welcomed him warmly as a leading Quaker.

The 'Quaker' vault. Thomas Penn, one of the Quaker's sons, but not himself a Quaker, had a large vault constructed beneath the nave of Penn Church, and four of his children and one of his brother Richard's, were laid to rest there between February 1753 and June 1766.[28] The children's ages ranged from 7 months to 12 years including twins who died six years apart. There was also an unrecorded sixth tiny coffin for a still-born child marked with a 'P'. The Rev. John Middleton, Vicar of Penn from 1787 to 1808, first came to Penn in March 1766 as the curate to the non-resident Vicar and so would probably have buried the last of the children in the vault. He reported in a letter dated August 9th 1802 that, 'Mr Penn made this Vault altho' he had no House or Land in the Parish. He wish'd much to make some purchases, but never could effect his purpose. He afterwards purchas'd a house and Estate at Stoke near Windsor, where his son at present resides, and where the family are now buried, a few only having been deposited in the Vault at Penn'.[29]   Only a church whose patron and vicar fully accepted the family's claim to kinship would have allowed him the privilege of such a major and disruptive undertaking.

Fig. 17   *Holy Trinity, Penn Church in the late 17th-century.*   A lithograph by W.F.Campbell of c.1800 taken from an earlier drawing or painting.

---

[27] *Penn Parish Register* shows no other possible candidates between 1650 and 1684
[28] *Penn Parish Register*
[29] Lysons Bucks Correspondence, BM, MS dept, Addn Cat 9411, f 205

> There is, also, under the Body of the Church, towards the Belfry, a large Vault built by the late Mr Penn, Proprietor of Pensilvania. Mr Penn made this Vault altho' he had no House or Land in the Parish. He wish'd much to make some purchases, but never c'd effect his purpose. He afterwards purchas'd a house and Estate at Stoke near Windsor, where his Son at present resides, and where the family are now buried, a few only having been deposited in the Vault at Penn.—

Fig. 18 *Vicar of Penn's letter of 1802,* about Thomas Penn making the vault and his search for property in Penn parish

Fig. 19 *1753 nave stone* marking the vault below in which William Penn's grandson, another William aged only 7 months, was the first child to be buried (Bucks Free Press Group)

Fig. 20 *Entrance to the vault in the north porch* when it was opened in 1987. Steps lead down to the vault (Beaconsfield Advertiser)

Fig. 21 *The 'Quaker' vault dug in 1753* The existence of the vault was remembered, but its whereabouts and entrance had been forgotten and was not re-discovered until March 1968 during work on the nave floor to cure dampness only a foot below floor-level. The Vicar had a hole drilled in the floor next to the stone memorial slab to William Penn, the first grandchild to be buried in 1753. He lowered a sort of periscope and having seen the vault the hole was enlarged and a camera lowered to take photographs. The entrance to the vault was found in the church porch, the vault entered and inscriptions on the six coffins examined. The vault was found to be of brick, 30ft x 10ft and 7ft high. It was then dry, but 21 years later, in Feb. 1987, when the author visited the vault with Earl Howe, the church architect and verger, it had recently been up to 5 ft deep in water. The wood of the coffins, apart from the lids, had all perished leaving the lead lining (Brian Cullip, 1987)

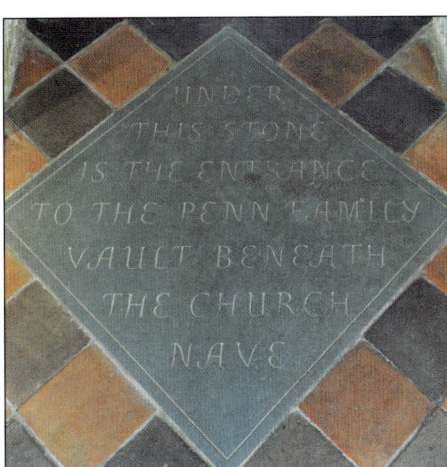

Fig. 22 *Inscribed vault stone* put in place in 1987 to mark the entrance to the vault in the north porch (Eddie Morton)

Fig. 23 *Coffin nameplate for Louisa Hannah* who died on '10th Day of June 1766, Aged 9 Years 10 Months & 19 Days'. She was the last child to be buried in the vault, joining her twin brother, another William, who had died in 1760 (Brian Cullip, 1987)

Fig. 24 *Thomas & Lady Juliana Penn.* Their marriage in 1751 – she was the daughter of the first Earl of Pomfret – marked the end of his association with the Quaker faith and afterwards he attended C of E services. Both he and his wife were extremely fond of their children whom he referred to as 'The Little People' and grieved for those who did not survive childhood

Fig. 25 *Coffin nameplate for a five year-old William Penn,* who died in 1760, held by the Rev. Oscar Muspratt, Vicar of Penn 1944-89 (Beaconsfield Advertiser)

Fig. 26 *The family of Thomas Penn,* by C.Turner after Reynolds. Taking ages from the family tree (Fig.29) suggests it was painted c.1762/3 when Juliana was 9 or 10; John 2 or 3; and Granville was the one year-old. The girl on the left must be Louisa, then about 7, who died three years later. They had already lost three brothers, including Louisa's twin brother, William. (NPG)

Attempt to purchase land in Penn. The Vicar's statement that Thomas Penn 'wish'd much to make some purchases of House or Land in the Parish, but never could effect his purpose' is now supported by documentary evidence. A letter addressed to 'The Hon. Tho. Penn Esq.' dated 7 May 1753, presumably from a surveyor, includes a rough sketch of a small 16 acre estate on Beacon Hill, Penn, which was for sale.[30] This was three months after the first child, Thomas's eldest son, had been buried in the vault under Penn Church.

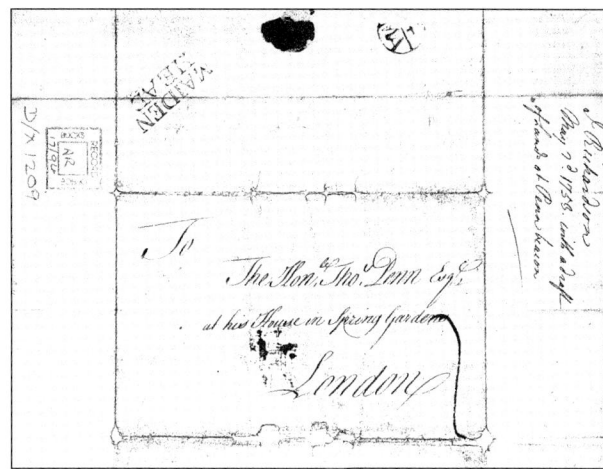

Fig. 27 *Letter from a surveyor to Thomas Penn in 1753* 'with a draft of lands at Penn beacon'

Penn Estate offered to Quaker Penns. Thomas Penn's youngest daughter Sophia used to relate that when her father was a very young man, she thought probably in about 1725, he received a letter from Roger Penn, the unmarried squire of Penn Manor 'saying he was going to make some settlement of his estate and if Thomas Penn would like to buy his property he would be ready to part with it. He desired, however, an immediate answer. Thomas Penn, pleased at this offer, wrote at once and accepted the proposal, but the servant entrusted with the letter never delivered it. When some days had elapsed, and old Mr Penn of Penn received no answer, he would not wait any longer, and settled it on the Curzon family'.[31] There may be another more convincing explanation. Roger Penn suffered from acute mood swings and drank heavily.[32] His last years were marked by great unhappiness. In 1728, his two surviving unmarried sisters, about 20 years older than him and effectively surrogate mothers who had probably been keeping house for him, both died within months of each other. Their brother died three years later and they are all buried close to each other in the chancel of Penn Church. Thomas Hearne, the well-known Oxford antiquary

---

[30] Bucks Record Office, AR17194 D/X1209
[31] Mrs Colquhoun Grant, *Quaker and Courtier. The life and work of William Penn*, John Murray (1907), p.238, fn2.
[32] Rev. Benjamin Robertshaw, Vicar of Penn 1716-28. His Memoirs are held in the Bucks Archaeological Society's library at Aylesbury, MISC/Box 1/32/56

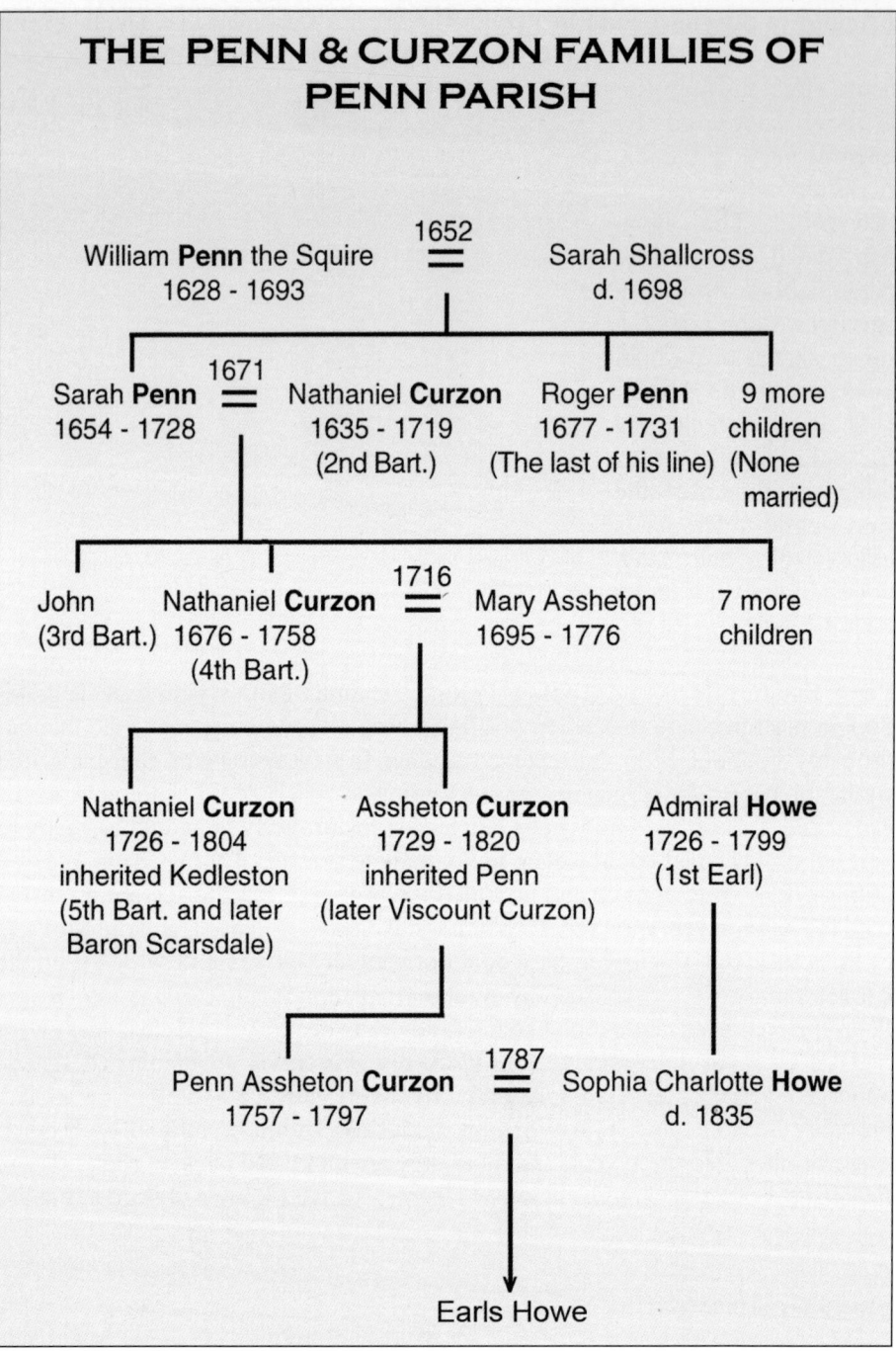

Fig. 28 *The Penn & Curzon families of Penn Parish*

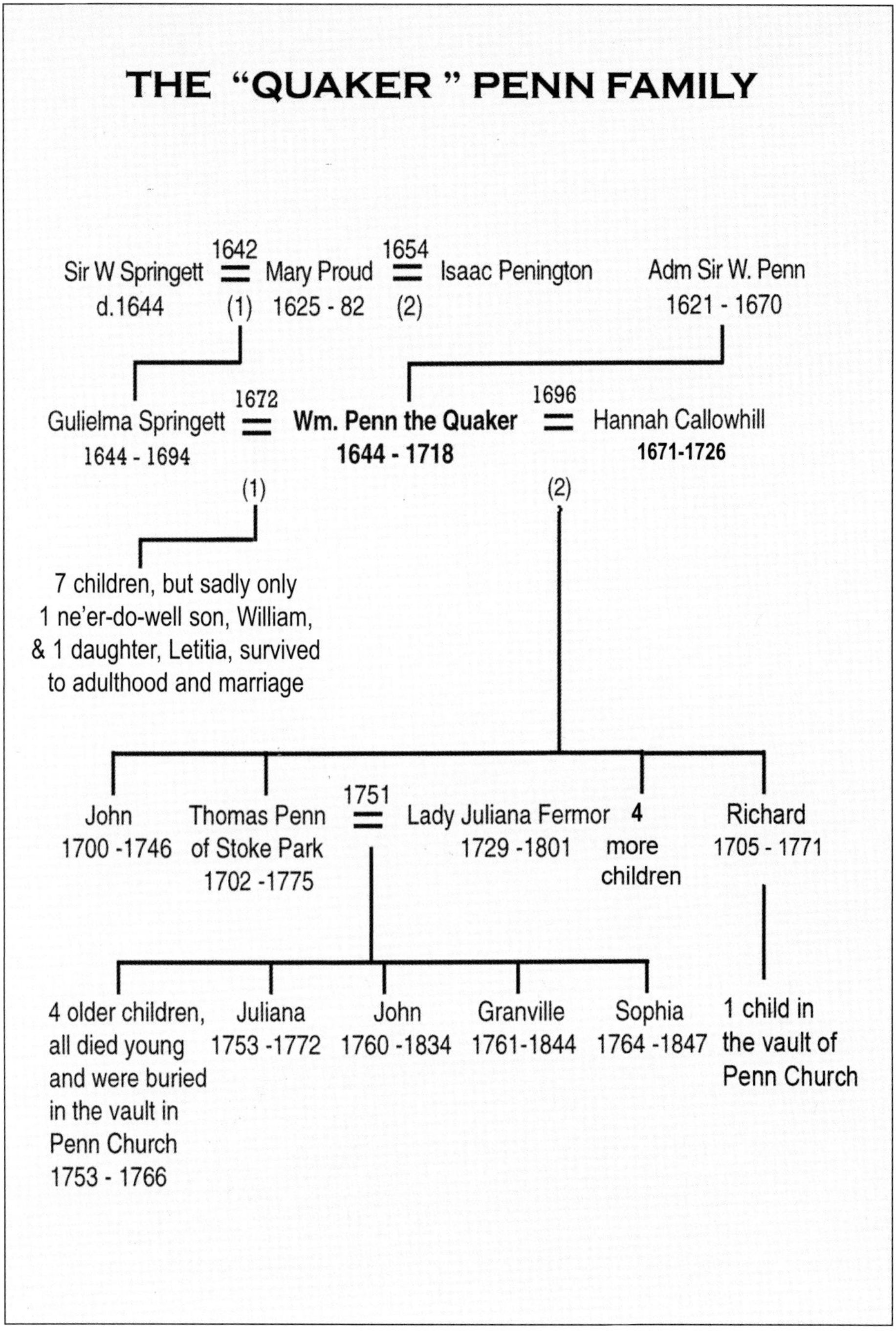

THE "QUAKER" PENN FAMILY

Sir W Springett =(1642)= Mary Proud =(1654)= Isaac Penington   Adm Sir W. Penn
d.1644   (1) 1625 - 82 (2)   1621 - 1670

Gulielma Springett =(1672)= **Wm. Penn the Quaker** =(1696)= Hannah Callowhill
1644 - 1694   1644 - 1718   1671-1726
        (1)   (2)

(1) 7 children, but sadly only 1 ne'er-do-well son, William, & 1 daughter, Letitia, survived to adulthood and marriage

(2)

John   Thomas Penn =(1751)= Lady Juliana Fermor   4 more   Richard
1700 -1746   of Stoke Park   1729 -1801   children   1705 - 1771
                  1702 -1775

4 older children,   Juliana   John   Granville   Sophia   1 child in
all died young   1753 -1772   1760 -1834   1761-1844   1764 -1847   the vault of
and were buried   Penn Church
in the vault in
Penn Church
1753 - 1766

Fig. 29 *The 'Quaker' Penn family*

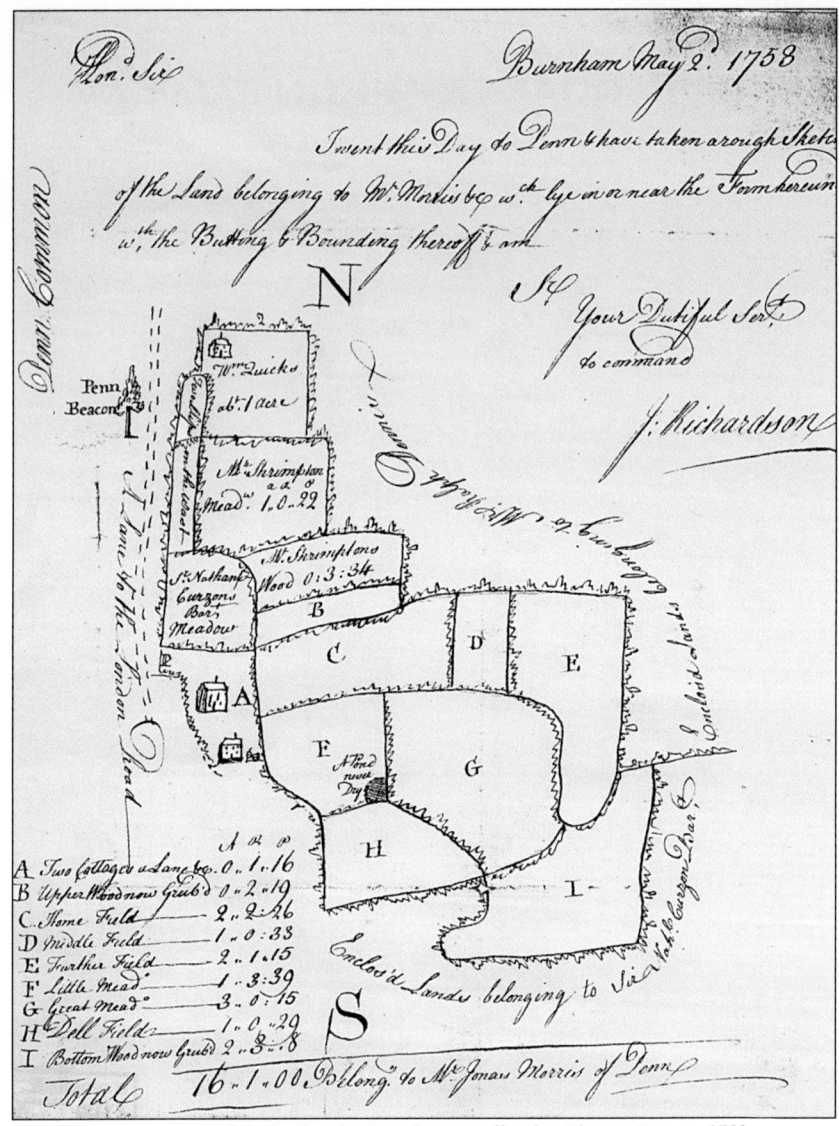

Fig. 30 *A rough sketch of the land at the Penn beacon offered to Thomas Penn in 1753*

and diarist, described him as 'a very honest gentleman and a very good scholar', but reported that he had lived for some considerable time almost altogether in his room, keeping no company, 'being as it were in a crazed condition'.[33]

---

[33] J.Gilbert Jenkins, *A history of the parish of Penn,* The St Catharine Press, London (1935), p.135. He quotes from Hearne's *Collections,* Oxford Historical Society, vols 6, 11

Evidence against a family link

There is thus no doubt whatsoever that in the 17th and 18th-centuries both families believed that they were related. However, no genealogical link of any kind has been established. Two of William Penn the Quaker's descendants have made detailed studies of the matter. His grandson, Granville Penn, added to his statement quoted above 'Relation of kindred was always mutually claimed and acknowledged ... but the genealogical connexion does not appear on record'.[34] Brigadier Hogg, the Quaker's great, great, great, great grandson, is uncompromising in his conclusion that no such relationship has ever existed. He makes several telling points:-

- Penn is not such an unusual surname and can be found at various times in about one third of English counties. By the 12th-century the name was already widely dispersed[35]
- He investigated five of the best known families called Penn in some detail, particularly the Penns of Minety in Wilts, and confirmed the Admiral's descent from William Penn, a yeoman of Minety, Wilts, who died in 1590 and whose father, John, died c.1560.[36]
- He found no evidence of any Welsh ancestry for the Quaker Penns, a suggestion according to some writers that came from William Penn the Quaker himself.[37] Perhaps William Penn had this in mind when he suggested New Wales as the name for his new lands in the Americas. The Buckinghamshire William Penn, for his part, would have remembered his younger brother, Gryffyth, and known about an earlier Gryffyth and David amongst his forbears. He would have known from the Manor Court Rolls, about a Gawine in the 15th-century.[38] He would also have known about the Shropshire branch of their family with the same coat of arms and an attested genealogy going back to the 13th-century, starting with a Sir William Penne.[39] Admiral Penn had discussion with the College of Arms about his own arms and would no doubt have discovered the Sir William Penne on the Welsh border. It can be seen that all these clues could have led both families to the erroneous belief that they were related through a Welsh border Penne connection.

---

[34] Granville Penn, *Memorials of the professional life and times of Sir William Penn, Knt*, London (1833), II, p.575
[35] Brigadier O.F.G. Hogg, *Further light on the ancestry of William Penn*, The Society of Genealogists (1964), pp.2, 3
[36] *Ibid*. pp. 9 et seq.
[37] *Ibid*., pp.2, 3
[38] J.Gilbert Jenkins, *A history of the parish of Penn*, St Catherine Press (1935), p.15. A Gavin le Penne signed a deed belonging to the borough of High Wycombe in 1443. Also, what appears to be an authentic Victorian summary of those parts of the Court Rolls which related to the Grove family between 1435 and 1685, seen by the author, suggests that Gawine Penne succeeded at some date after 1435.
[39] Brigadier O.F.G.Hogg, *op.cit.*, p.8

Fig. 31 *William Penn meets Gulielma Springett and Isaac Penington.* This would have been in 1667 when both were aged 23, but this is an oil painting with no known provenance and is probably a Victorian painter using his imagination. It makes a pleasing image (Woodbrooke Quaker Studies Centre)

Fig.32 *Lady Mary Springett (1625-82),* mother of Gulielma Springett and later wife of Isaac Penington (Pennsbury Manor, Pennsylvania)

Fig. 33 *Hannah Penn (1671-1726).* She was William Penn's second wife. Very uncertain provenance (Courtesy of Friends Historical Library of Swarthmore College)

- The similarity in the family arms was because Admiral Penn borrowed those of the Penns of Bucks and 'differenced' them by adding a crescent, denoting either a second son or a recognised cadet branch of the family. However he had no authority to do this since the College of Arms never granted any arms to the Admiral or his son and recorded the family as 'non-armigerous'.[40]

The Admiral's Arms

This last point is of particular interest. The Admiral was first knighted by Henry Cromwell in 1658.[41] His knighthood was confirmed by King Charles in 1660 and subsequently registered by the Herald's Office, where he was noted as, 'Sir William Penne of ———.' It may be that the Admiral never pursued the question of arms because he was apparently expecting a peerage which would require different arms, an expectation frustrated by his son becoming a Quaker.[42] It may be that he was unable to meet the strict College of Arms requirement for proof of his claimed Buckinghamshire connection and so quietly dropped the matter, preferring to continue his unofficial usage. The arms used on his monument were prepared by one of the leading Herald Painters of the day and includes a crescent indicating a cadet branch.[43] For nearly a century, whilst Pennsylvania was still a province of England, its seals were those of William Penn and his sons and grandsons who succeeded him as Proprietor. However, since the Declaration of Independence, in 1776, neither the state seals nor coat of arms have carried the Penn arms.

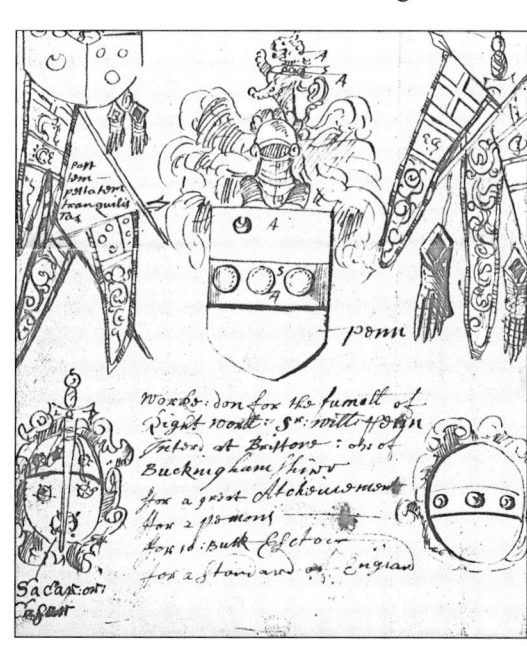

Fig. 34 *Sketches by the Herald Painter* of the arms to be used on Admiral Sir William Penn's monument in St Mary Redcliffe, Bristol (British Library)

---

[40] *Ibid.*, p.35.
[41] Robert Latham and William Mathews, *The Diary of Samuel Pepys*, (1983), Vol IX, p.312
[42] Mrs Colquhoun Grant, op.cit., pp. 39, 40. The Admiral understood that it was likely that a peerage was awaiting his acceptance under the title of Viscount Weymouth. In 1660 he had become MP for Weymouth
[43] BM Addn 26683, f516b, has sketches by the Herald Painter of the arms used on the monument in Bristol

The Peningtons and Gulielma Springett

One of the most notable of the few Quakers from the local gentry was Isaac Penington of the Grange, Chalfont St Peter. His father had been Lord Mayor of London in 1642/43, and was one of Parliament's judges who had condemned Charles I to death in 1649, for which he died in the Tower a year after the restoration of Charles II in 1660. This made his son a particular target of persecution. Isaac Penington was imprisoned six times for a total of five years between 1660 and 1670 for his Quaker beliefs and eventually his estates were sequestrated. He married Lady Mary Springett in 1654 and so became stepfather to her curiously named daughter, Gulielma Maria Posthuma, who was the posthumous daughter of Sir William Springett, a Captain in the Parliamentary army, who had died at the siege of Arundel. Gulielma is a Latinisation of her father's name.[44]

John Aubrey has left this flattering description of Gulielma – 'virtuous, generous, wise, humble, plaine (i.e.frank); generally beloved for those good qualities and one more – the great cures she does, having great skill in physic and surgery, which she freely bestows. She early espoused the same (religious) way, about anno 1657 (when she was 13). She was a great fortune to her husband being worth *de claro* above 10,000 pounds'.[45] Gulielma was a noted beauty with a good estate and with many very eligible rivals for her affections. It is thought she first met William Penn in 1667 after his return from Ireland and the few surviving letters show that he was writing to her by 1668. He took no small pride in being her choice. In a later tribute to her memory he described her as his 'entire and constant friend, of a more than common capacity and greater modesty and humility, yet most equal and undaunted in danger'.[46]

Isaac Penington was put in Aylesbury gaol in 1665, having made an enemy of the Earl of Bridgewater by refusing to address him as 'My Lord' or sign letters as 'Your Humble Servant'. The Earl declared he should "lie in prison till he would rot". Shortly afterwards, the Peningtons were ejected from his estate at the Grange and Mary Penington with Gulielma took a small house near Aylesbury to be close to her husband. After Isaac Penington's release in 1668, his wife lost, in her turn, a large part of her own estate by refusing to take an oath in court. They then endured many tiring moves looking for a house near Chalfont, close to understanding friends who would sympathise with their poverty which they found hard after being used to great plenty. 'They had a

---

[44] Beatrice Saxon Snell (ed.), *Quaker Minute Book for the Upperside of Bucks, 1669-1690*, Bucks Arch. Soc. (1937), I, pp. vii, viii
[45] John Aubrey, *Brief Lives*, Anthony Powell (ed.), London (1949), p.361
[46] William Braithwaite, *The Second period of Quakerism*, Macmillan (1921), p.75

sense of our former condition, and were compassionate of us; we being in their sight so stripped...but rather wondered of us that we were able to live so decently and pay everyone their own.'[47] They nearly bought a house in Beaconsfield but eventually decided to buy and extend Woodside House in Amersham, at first in an agony of mind over the expense, but eventually with pleasure and satisfaction. There was much to repair and extend so it took nearly four years, apparently starting in 1669, so it was not ready until the end of 1672 or early in 1673.[48]

After his father died, in September 1670, William Penn visited Buckinghamshire to see Gulielma and his other friends, but a detailed account of the Penns and Peningtons concludes that 'neither letter nor narrative tell us of his visits'.[49] Again, after his release from Newgate prison in August 1671, 'he lost no time till he saw his beloved Guli'. Their marriage settlement was made in 1671, probably about this time. [50] He then went on missionary visits to Holland, some German states and East Anglia before returning again to Gulielma, probably in December, but again 'no family documents are forthcoming relative to the period from his return from the continent to the end of the year after his marriage in April 1672'. His biographer, William Hepworth Dixon, is quoted as saying

Fig. 35 *King John's Farm, Chorleywood* where William Penn and Gulielma were married on 4 April 1672. It was then a Quaker Meeting House. (Library of the Society of Friends, London)

Fig. 36 *Basing House in Rickmansworth* which William Penn and Gulielma rented for the first five years of their marriage (Library of the Society of Friends, London)

---

[47] Maria Webb, *The Penns and Peningtons of the 17th-century*, (1891), pp. 162-3
[48] *Ibid.*, pp.164-8
[49] *Ibid.*, pp.211
[50] BM MS3 Egerton MS 2168, Family of Penn temp Chas I – 1734. These papers were inspected in the British Library but unfortunately there is only an inventory recording the existence of the marriage settlement of 1671, but nothing more

that William Penn posted down to Bucks to see Gulielma and the Peningtons and 'seems to have passed a considerable time, dallying with the blissful days of courtship, and slowly making preparations for his marriage'. He rented Basing House at Rickmansworth which was being made ready for Guli's reception.[51]

Evidence of the Quaker presence in Penn

There are seven separate references which are summarised in Fig.16. In chronological order these are:

- Entries in William Penn's Irish Journal record his visit with Gulielma, to Penn Street, presumably to Penn House, on 18 Sep 1669, before they were married. They would have been visiting William Penn's 'cousins' at Penn House in Penn Street, a small hamlet of cottages which had grown up outside the gates of Penn House. The journal confirms that the Peningtons were living at Amersham at that time.[52]

Fig. 37 *Gulielma Penn,* William Penn's first wife. Uncertain provenance (Frontispiece, Maria Webb's Penns and Peningtons)

- A letter headed, '**Pen** 16 -5 month 1670' (i.e. 16 July), from Gulielma and Mary Pennington to William Penn, who was in Ireland, in which they report that Isaac Pennington was once more in gaol and that 'deare G F (George Fox) was heare att two of our meettings and they were very large' (see Fig.38 opposite). [53] This is the only surviving letter from Gulielma to William Penn before her marriage.

---

[51] Maria Webb, *op.cit.*, pp.220-1
[52] See p.16 and fn. 24 and related text above it
[53] Mary Maples Dunn & Richard S.Dunn (eds.), *The Papers of William Penn*, University of Pennsylvania Press (1981), Vol 1, p.156. Isaac Penington stayed in Reading Gaol until Charles II's Declaration of Indulgence on 15 March 1672 extended toleration to Protestant religious dissenters and allowed imprisoned Quakers to be freed –just in time for Gulielma's wedding on 4 April 1672 at which he signed the marriage certificate as one of the witnesses

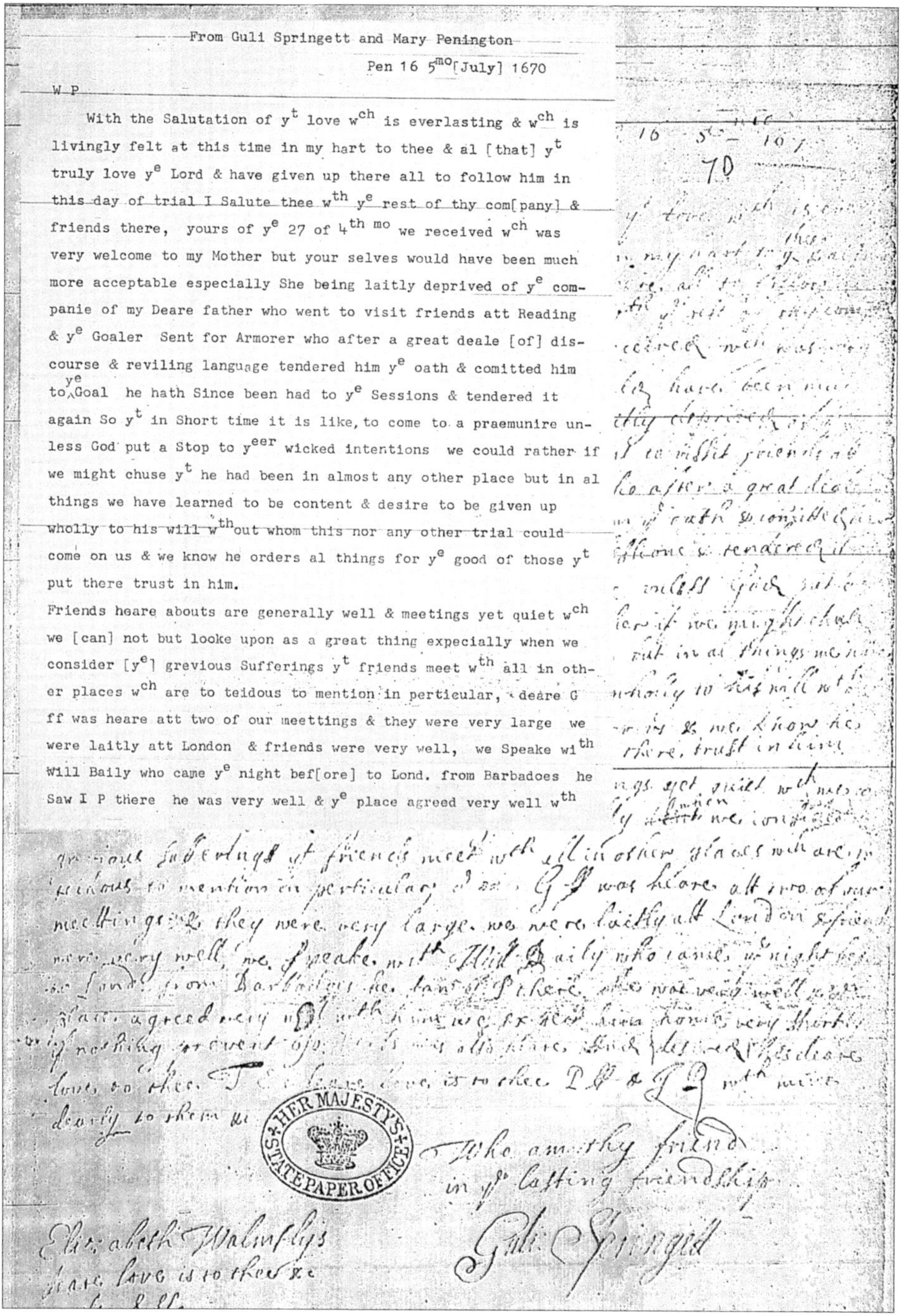

From Guli Springett and Mary Penington

Pen 16 5mo [July] 1670

W P

With the Salutation of yt love wch is everlasting & wch is livingly felt at this time in my hart to thee & al [that] yt truly love ye Lord & have given up there all to follow him in this day of trial I Salute thee wth ye rest of thy com[pany] & friends there, yours of ye 27 of 4th mo we received wch was very welcome to my Mother but your selves would have been much more acceptable especially She being laitly deprived of ye companie of my Deare father who went to visit friends att Reading & ye Goaler Sent for Armorer who after a great deale [of] discourse & reviling language tendered him ye oath & comitted him to ye Goal he hath Since been had to ye Sessions & tendered it again So yt in Short time it is like, to come to a praemunire unless God put a Stop to yeer wicked intentions we could rather if we might chuse yt he had been in almost any other place but in al things we have learned to be content & desire to be given up wholly to his will wthout whom this nor any other trial could come on us & we know he orders al things for ye good of those yt put there trust in him.

Friends heare abouts are generally well & meetings yet quiet wch we [can] not but looke upon as a great thing expecially when we consider [ye] grevious Sufferings yt friends meet wth all in other places wch are to teidous to mention in perticular, deare G ff was heare att two of our meettings & they were very large we were laitly att London & friends were very well, we Speake with Will Baily who came ye night bef[ore] to Lond. from Barbadoes he Saw I P there he was very well & ye place agreed very well wth

HER MAJESTY'S STATE PAPER OFFICE

Who am thy friend
in ye lasting friendship

Guli Springett

Elizabeth Walmslys
deare love is to thee &c

Fig. 38 *Letter from Gulielma to William Penn,* dated Pen 16-5mo (July) 1670. He was in Ireland. The transcript is superimposed on the original, very poor quality, microfilm of Gulielma's letter. Microfilm no. XI/7814 with copyright Historical Society of Pennsylvania (Library of the Society of Friends, London)

Fig. 39 *Holy Trinity, Penn Church, 11th Nov 2007* – showing the flags still put out every year on Remembrance Day to remember the fallen in WW II. Six U.S. flags remember the crew of an American bomber which crashed at the nearby Lude Farm in 1944. Their names are read out every year with our own.(Eddie Morton)

Fig. 40 *Penn House, Penn Street* - a large part of the Elizabethan house was pulled down in 1760 and only the left hand side retains any earlier features. (Eddie Morton)

- A pamphlet called, *Seasonable Caveat against Popery*, was first written by W.P. in Ireland in early 1670, but a second edition, printed in London, has a preface, 'W.P. **Penn**, Buckinghamshire, the 23rd of the 11th Moneth 1670'. That is 23 Jan 1671, new style.[54]

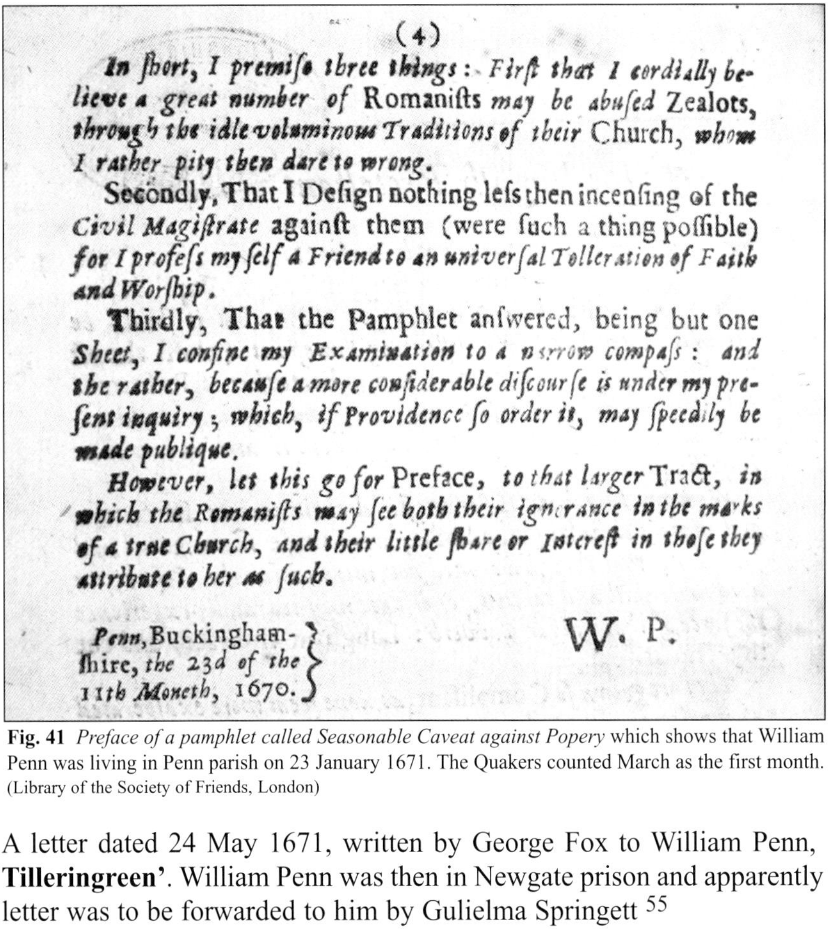

> (4)
>
> In *fhort, I premife three things*: Firft *that I cordially believe a great number* of Romanists *may be abufed* Zealots, *through the idle voluminous Traditions of their* Church, *whom I rather pity then dare to wrong.*
>
> Secondly, That I Defign nothing lefs then incenfing of the Civil Magiftrate againft them (were fuch a thing poffible) *for I profefs my felf a Friend to an univerfal Tolleration of Faith and Worfhip.*
>
> Thirdly, That the Pamphlet anfwered, being but one Sheet, I confine *my Examination to a narrow compafs: and the rather, becaufe a more confiderable difcourfe is under my prefent inquiry; which, if Providence fo order it, may fpeedily be made publique.*
>
> However, let this go for Preface, *to that larger* Tract, *in which the Romanists may fee both their ignorance in the marks of a true Church, and their little fhare or intereft in thofe they attribute to her as fuch.*
>
> *Penn*, Buckingham-   W. P.
> fhire, *the* 23d *of the*
> 11th *Moneth*, 1670.

Fig. 41 *Preface of a pamphlet called* Seasonable Caveat against Popery *which shows that William Penn was living in Penn parish on 23 January 1671. The Quakers counted March as the first month.*
(Library of the Society of Friends, London)

- A letter dated 24 May 1671, written by George Fox to William Penn, 'att **Tilleringreen**'. William Penn was then in Newgate prison and apparently the letter was to be forwarded to him by Gulielma Springett [55]

---

[54] Edwin B.Bonner & David Fraser (eds.), *The Papers of William Penn*, University of Pennsylvania (1996), Vol 5, p. 105. The editors noted that when arranging this second edition WP indicated 'that he was at the village of Penn in Buckinghamshire, near where Gulielma Springett and the Peningtons resided, at the time the arrangements were made'. This comment would seem to wrongly assume that Tyler End Green and Penn were adjacent villages when in fact Tyler End Green is a hamlet of Penn.

[55] Mary Maples Dunn & Richard S.Dunn (eds.), *op.cit.*, Vol 1. p.208. George Fox was an indefatigable letter writer. WP knew him very well, 'having been with him for weeks and months together on divers occasions…by night and by day, by sea and by land, in this and in foreign countries'. Tillering Green, Tiler End Green and now Tylers Green are all variants of the same name

- The Quaker Monthly Meeting Book records on 7 Feb 1672 the first declaration of the intention of marriage between 'William Penn of Walthamstow in the county of Essex and Gulielma Maria Springett of **Tiler End Green** in the parish of Penn in the County of Bucks'. 'Consent and approbation' was given at the following Meeting on 6 March 1672.[56]

- The wedding itself took place at King John's Farm, Chorley Wood on 4 April 1672 and the marriage certificate describes the bride as Gulielma Maria Springett of **Penn** in the county of Bucks.[57]

The apparently unquestioned assumption hitherto, has been that the Peningtons and Gulielma occupied 'Berrie' House in Amersham for all the four years that Woodside House was being extended from 1669 to 1672/3, but there seems to be no evidence of their being in Amersham after September 1669. On the other hand, there is this clear documentary evidence that they were living at Tyler End Green by July 1670 and were still there in April 1672. The Peningtons may well have stayed on after Gulielma's marriage until Woodside House was ready for them at the end of 1672 or early 1673.

This misreading of the historical record seems to have been based on an uncritical acceptance of the assumption made by Maria Webb in her much quoted, *The Penns and Peningtons of the Seventeenth Century* (1867), although, as we have seen, she made it clear that there were no family letters or documents covering that period.[58] There are indeed many gaps in the documentary record, particularly in the 1660s and 1670s. The only surviving letter from Gulielma to William Penn before 1679 is the one of July 1670 quoted above. William Penn's Irish Journal records him sending 70 letters and receiving 25 in ten months of 1669/70. Only one incoming and one outgoing letter still exist. It is estimated that no more than 5% of the letters he wrote and received from 1644 to 1679 has survived.[59]

It is interesting to note that the Peningtons were in contact with Quakers from Penn parish before they moved there. In mid 1669, when Thomas Ellwood escorted Gulielma to stay with her uncle in Kent and to visit her tenants, her

---

[56] Beatrice S. Snell (ed.), *Quaker Minute Book for the Upperside of Bucks 1669-1690*, Bucks Arch.Soc (1937), pp.12, 13. Both meetings were held at Thomas Ellwood's house, Hunger Hill, at Larkins Green in Coleshill parish. The Quakers met there because it was an outlying part of Hertfordshire and so safe from persecution by the Bucks authorities. The Minute Book records only the business of the Upperside group of Particular Meetings

[57] Mary Maples Dunn & Richard S.Dunn (eds.) *op.cit.*, Vol 1, pp. 238-9

[58] See fns 49, 51 and associated text.

[59] Mary Maples Dunn & Richard S.Dunn (eds.), *op.cit.*, Vol 1, pp.10, 11

groom was 'honest John Gigger' who was a Quaker from Penn.[60] In 1673, William Penn contributed generously to a fund to rescue John Gigger Snr from debt.[61] The Quaker Minute Book reveals a nest of Quakers in Penn in the decade or so after 1671 with mention of eight different families.[62] These local Quaker families, the Quaker sympathies of some of the Squire's family and their assumed kinship with William Penn would have made Penn a far more welcoming place than many others for the harassed Peningtons.

The house in Tiler End Green

What can we say about the house in which they were living at Tyler End Green in the parish of Penn? We know from the deeds in the County Record Office in Aylesbury and from mid-18th-century maps (see Fig.47) that there was a medieval house of some size with about 4 acres of garden overlooking Tylers Green common near the large pond.[63] The deeds show that from 1669 the property was twice mortgaged and it was let to a succession of short-stay tenants, starting with a Robert Danvers Esq, until it was sold in 1680. There is no record of any other house in Tyler End Green that was of the size and quality expected for people of the social class of the Peningtons even in their reduced circumstances,[64] and we know it must have been fairly big if it accommodated the 'very large' Quaker meetings reported by Gulielma when George Fox visited in July 1670. This was the year before Quaker meetings started to be held at Jordans. The Peningtons' name does not appear on the deeds, but the house may have been sub-let or perhaps they could have stayed there as guests of a sympathetic tenant or owner.

Although Isaac Penington's estate had been confiscated, his wife still had property in Kent and noted with relief that her rents were coming in steadily. Theirs was a comparatively genteel poverty and Gulielma, who was a wealthy woman in her own right from her father's inheritance, travelled with a maid or a groom.[65] William Penn would anyway have surely made sure they were not

---

[60] Maria Webb, *The Penns and Peningtons*, London (1891), pp.180-3; and Beatrice S. Snell (ed.), *op.cit.*, p. 9
[61] Beatrice S. Snell (ed.), *op.cit.*, pp.19, 21, 25
[62] 1671, John Gigger; 1673, John Gigger the Elder; 1676, Nicholas Horton, Martha Blake; 1677, Mary Kingham; 1678, Frances Goulder, William Goulder; 1679, Timothy Anthony; Ann Higgins; 1680, Henry Higgins; 1684, Thomas Martin. Since the Minute Book recorded only marriages, personal problems, financial matters, and so on, there are likely to have been more families unrecorded
[63] BRO R/136/79/8. There is a long series of deeds starting in 1669. Jeffery's map of 1770 shows a house owned by Boucher Esq. The deeds show Dr William Bouchier bought the house from the Baker family in 1770
[64] *Records of Bucks*, V, p.274. The Vicar of Penn writing in c.1883, also came to the same conclusion
[65] Maria Webb, *op.cit.*, pp.167, 176, 180

However, the Bodleian painting does show a house of the age and size that we might expect for the 'Quaker' house' in its enlarged Baker years. Descriptions of old paintings and portraits were often added generations later and were not infrequently inaccurate and confused. This may well be such a case, recording the house as destroyed in 1818 rather than 1822 and it may well have been badly damaged by fire since the Baker Diary shows a constant preoccupation with fire precautions and records a serious fire in the kitchen chimney in 1698 (see Fig.42) and in the brewhouse in 1700.[70] Whilst we cannot say with any certainty that this was the house to which the Peningtons had moved by July 1670, it does seem to be a promising candidate.

Twentieth-century disputes

The Vicars' war of words

No one questioned the validity of the claim to kinship between the Quaker Penns and the Penns of the parish for nearly a century after William Penn died and when Granville Penn concluded that 'no genealogical connection appears on record', it was not of particular moment. It only seems to have become contentious at the very start of the 20th-century with rivalry between two vicars for the ear of their patron, the 4th Earl Howe. When his father died in 1900, the new Earl chose the long-serving Vicar of Tylers Green to officiate at the funeral in preference to the newly-arrived Vicar of Penn. The resentful Vicar of Penn gate-crashed the funeral and his Tylers Green colleague asked the local policeman to have him taken in charge for causing a disturbance.

Fig. 43 The Rev. Ashley Spencer, Vicar of Tylers Green 1883-1918 (Postcard from Harold Wheeler)

In 1913, this unhappy relationship burst into flames once more in what was described by the local newspaper as 'an exceptionally interesting action' heard at the Bucks Assizes before a special jury. The Vicar of Tylers Green accused the Vicar of Penn of serious libel in the form of anonymous letters and postcards

---

[70] Miles Green & Pat Sharp, *op.cit.*, pp. 6, 11

Fig. 44 *The old house in Tyler End Green* where it is suggested the Peningtons and Gulilma Springett were living for two years, 1670-72. It overlooked the pond and open common. (Bodleian Library, Oxford)

Fig. 45 *Site of the old house overlooking Tylers Green Common today* (Eddie Morton)

sent to him, the Archdeacon, Sir Philip Rose and others, signed with such descriptions as 'A Well-Wisher' or 'Disgusted Parishioner' These messages said the Tylers Green Vicar's drinking habits had long been the talk of the whole neighbourhood and he had taken money sent him for the Church for his own private purposes; that he was 'a liar, drunkard and thief'; and that he was 'a drunken little devil' and conducted services whilst under the influence and played cards after Sunday evening services.

Under the questioning of a highly amused judge, two examples of the kind of unsuitable behaviour typical of the Vicar of Penn were given by the King's Counsel representing the Vicar of Tylers Green. One of these was forcing himself into the funeral and the other that he had gone to America and collected a sum of money for the restoration of Penn Church under false pretences claiming that the village of Penn was connected with William Penn the Quaker, the founder of Pennsylvania.[71] In fact there was no such connection and the Vicar of Tylers Green had written pointing this out. An argument on this then followed, which led to the Judge declaring the visit to Pennsylvania immaterial to the case. He concluded, "I do not know how many Penns there are in Penn but there is certainly a pen in Penn Parish which has penned letters that might have been unpenned". It took the jury only 18 minutes to find the Vicar of Penn guilty and he was required to pay £400 - a very large sum of money in those days, sufficient to buy a very nice house in Knotty Green - as well as the costs.[72]

Pennsylvania visits and visitors

This argument has continued into modern times with the Rev. Oscar Muspratt, the long-serving Vicar of Penn from 1945 to 1989, absolutely determined to prove that William Penn the Quaker was from the same family as the Penns of Penn Parish.[73] Every Pennsylvanian milestone was celebrated in Penn Church, often with radio and TV coverage to the States, with messages exchanged with Philadelphia and with a representative of the US military or from the US

---

[71] *Penn Parish Register* records a very active vicar. A major repair of the church tower and nave roof was carried out in 1903 by public subscription and a later church parish magazine records that funds from America helped to pay for them

[72] *South Bucks Free Press*, 17 Oct 1913

[73] The Rev.Oscar Muspratt, *William Penn's family saga*, Penn PCC (1984). His arguments include the unexpected claim that the motto 'Justice, Mercy', apparently used in Pennsylvania's seal and coat of arms before 1776, derives from the Doom painting (Justice) which used to hang above the chancel arch in Penn Church and from the Virgin Mary (Mercy) who would have been at the foot of the Rood Cross which hung below the Doom. But the Doom and Rood were part of the medieval church and both disappeared at the Reformation, a century before the time we are considering. There is no record of any motto used by the Buckinghamshire Penns and WP used 'Dum clavum teneam' (see fn.23 above)

Embassy. 1968 was the 250th anniversary of William Penn's death; 1969, his 325th birthday; 1976, the 200th anniversary of the United States when Mr Muspratt was invited to a service in Westminster Abbey; 1981, the 300th anniversary of Pennsylvania when the Governor sent a Pennsylvania flag for the church. Whenever the Lambeth Conference brought the Bishops of Pennsylvania or Delaware to England, they were invited to Penn and in memory of the first visit in 1948, a window was dedicated in the Lady Chapel.

Mr Muspratt was invited three times to Philadelphia as an official guest. In 1962, by the Bishop of Pennsylvania to whom he presented a solid silver replica key to Penn Church (which is apparently now in Christ Church, Philadelphia). He met the Governor, was presented with the key to the city of Pittsburgh, opened a session of the Senate with prayers, and made nine broadcasts and two TV interviews. In 1969, he and the Earl & Countess Howe were invited as guests of the Mayor of Philadelphia. In 1982, the Vicar was the only English member of the Mayor's official party on the QE2 following William Penn's voyage across the Atlantic and sailing up the Delaware River. On every visit there was a programme of meetings, interviews, lectures and dinner parties. He addressed the State Legislature, visited the Senate and the UN and took every opportunity to advance his argument that his many years of researches had proved that the parish of Penn was William Penn's ancestral home. Copies of his researches were widely distributed.[74]

Fig. 46 *Bishop of Pennsylvania window* in the Lady Chapel of Holy Trinity Church, Penn. It commemorates his first visit in 1948 after a Lambeth Conference (Eddie Morton)

---

[74] Mr Muspratt arranged for copies of the Penn Parish church magazine from 1937 to 1989 to be bound in four volumes. He gives a full account in them of all his activities and the conclusions he drew from his researches, as well as commenting on current world events. It is a very valuable record of his 45 years in office

Fig. 47 *Jefferys map 1770.* Red arrows mark the Tyler End Green house where it is suggested that the Peningtons and Gulielma were living, and Penn House.
Penn Church is shown just above the second 'n' of Penn.
Rayners Farm is just below the 'B' of Boucher
(Bucks Archaeological Society)

Fig. 48 *Almshouses built in 1831 opposite Penn Church.* They were demolished in 1967 to make way for the Penn Mead apartments which can be seen on the right (Church archive)

It was all heady stuff and he returned to Philadelphia on private visits for the next four years. A Penn-Pennsylvania Fellowship, known as the Penn Trust, was launched in 1963 with the overall aim of 'preserving and perpetuating the historical character and associations of the ancient village of Penn'. It opened with a large local bequest of £40,000, but it is not clear that any funds were attracted from Pennsylvania. A major rift in the village was caused by proposals under the Trust's auspices in 1965 to create a new Penn Centre with a large new William Penn Memorial Hall. This involved demolishing the old almshouses opposite the church, as well as the former school, already by then converted to a Church Hall, in order to build the new Hall, a 3-storey block of 22 small flats and apartments for 'distressed' gentlefolk, and parking for 60 cars, The proposals were designed by Sir Hugh Casson, one of the leading architects of his day and a cousin of the Vicar's. They also included a recommendation for a relief road for the B474 to take traffic away from the village.

The general verdict, putting the uncertain historical premise to one side, was that it was far too ambitious a project, too expensive, too grandiose, too disruptive.[75] A hostile public meeting shouted Sir Hugh down and the plan was withdrawn. The Penn & Tylers Green Society, headed by leading parishioners, was set up as a guardian for the future.[76] The only part of the plan which was implemented was the replacement of the almshouses which were judged not worthy of repair and were replaced in 1967 by eight small, but well-designed apartments known as Penn Mead, which have proved a success. They presumably take their name from the famous Penn-Mead trial concerning William Penn the Quaker.[77]

---

[75] It was described by a leading opponent of the scheme as 'a cross between an enormous bird cage and the elephant house at the zoo, absolutely out of scale and totally out of keeping with the pretty cottages, the pub and the church'

[76] Earl Howe was President of the new Society. By an interesting coincidence, one of the Vice-Presidents was the Earl of Ranfurly, a descendant of William Penn via Thomas Penn's daughter, Sophia. Others were John Betjeman, the future Poet Laureate; Rupert Davies, the actor; Oliver Millar, the future Surveyor of the Queen's Pictures; Alison Uttley, the writer; and Elizabeth Taylor, the novelist

[77] This account is taken from the church magazines and from the archive of the Penn Trust held locally, courtesy of the current Chairman, Christopher White

A glass screen in the porch of Penn Church

A more recent controversy, which ran for three years from 1984, was caused by the proposal to place a glass screen in the main north porch of Penn Church designed to both keep out draughts and to celebrate the family connection between William Penn the Quaker and the Penns of Penn Parish and their Curzon descendants. It is a very fine piece of craftsmanship[78], but quite apart from the disputed family relationship it represents, it is not as historically appropriate or accurate as it might have been. The Sir William Penn depicted on the screen is not contemporary with the Quaker or even with his father the Admiral, but is the grandfather of the Squire William we have been discussing and had died before the Quaker was born. He was not a knight and his wife Martha was not a Lady.[79]

Fig. 49 *Glass screen in porch of Penn Church.* (Based on a drawing photographed and amended by Eddie Morton)

---

[78] The screen is described in the fund-raising booklet and in the Penn Parish church magazine as designed by Penelope Adamson, the church's architect, with modifications by Sir Hugh Casson, former President of the Royal Academy; with the figures drawn by Michael Farrar Bell, former President of the British Society of Master Glass Painters; and engraving by Rufus Ide & Co, the firm which made the famous west windows in Coventry Cathedral

[79] The depiction of William and Martha closely follows that on their brasses on the floor of the south aisle near the Lady Chapel and they were presumably chosen to represent the Penn family for that reason because the only images for the more relevant William Penn the Squire (1628-93) and his wife, Sarah, are less conveniently found in a painting in Penn House

The Sara Penn (1700-1730) depicted is not identifiable in any local record.[80] The figure of William Penn is based on the 37-foot-high bronze statue on top of City Hall in Philadelphia which was put up in 1894.[81] The fund-raising booklet estimated the cost of the screen at 40,000 American dollars and asked for cheques to be made payable to the Penn Pennsylvania Fellowship in the UK or to American Friends of Historic British Churches in the USA. It was this high cost and the radical change to a medieval porch which fuelled objections rather than the historical inaccuracies which were not realised at the time.

Mr Muspratt reported that at one point there had been the strong possibility that the Queen might have dedicated the screen since it so uniquely expressed Britain's share in the 200th anniversary of the U.S. constitution, which borrowed significantly from William Penn's constitution for Pennsylvania. In the event, dedication was by the Bishop of Oxford and American involvement was confined to messages of goodwill from several Governors and their Ambassador in London.[82]

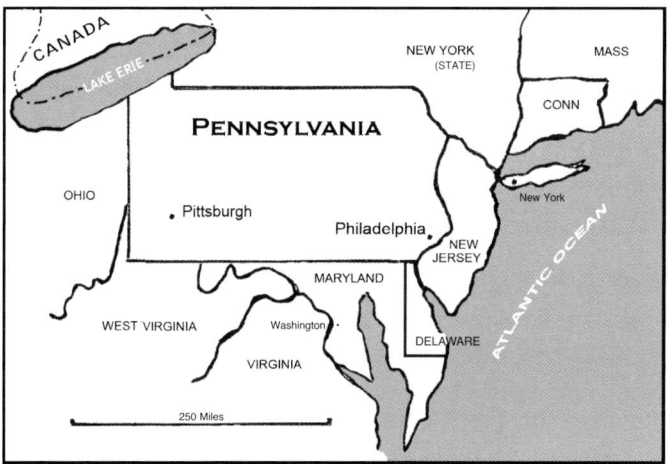

Fig. 50 *Map of Pennsylvania* (Tracing amended and elaborated by Eddie Morton)

---

[80] The illustration in the fund-raising booklet shows a Sarah Penn (1654-1727), who was a great-granddaughter of William & Martha. She would indeed have known the Quaker well. She married Nathaniel Curzon in 1671, the year before William Penn married Gulielma, and is therefore an ancestress of the present Earl Howe. Her dress on the screen - and the dog - seem to have been taken from a family portrait in Penn House (see Fig.11). Quite why her name and dates were changed on the screen itself to an unknown Sara is not clear

[81] The statue is apparently the tallest in the world that stands on top of a building. City Hall is 548 feet high with the statue, which looks out towards his house, Pennsbury Manor in Bucks County

[82] Oscar Muspratt put his heart and soul into Penn Church. He said it was his life's work and he led from the front reporting that he had put over £20,000 of his own money into various projects and committed every penny of his stipend after his 80th birthday to realising his aims. He was tireless in identifying projects and absolutely determined in raising funds and achieving his objective despite set-backs. His 45 years were marked by occasional controversies, but they left the fabric of the church greatly enriched

Conclusion
Taking the three main themes of the investigation:

Kinship – There has long been abundant evidence that the two families believed they were related, and this has been supplemented by the discovery of the Quaker's visit to Penn House and the specific evidence of Thomas Penn's interest in buying property in the parish. One can quite see that both families had good reason to welcome the idea of kinship. It was almost certainly the two contemporary William Penns who first met each other. The Admiral, born in 1621, and the Sheriff of Bucks, born in 1628; both successful at an early age during the Commonwealth; struck by the coincidence of having the same Christian name and surname, sharing perhaps a romantic belief in a Welsh border origin of their family name; the one a descendant of a yeoman, gratified to be associated with a family of such long lineage, the other flattered by the association with a famous Admiral. However, they were mistaken since genealogical enquiry points firmly to a separate ancestry.

The Peningtons in Tyler End Green - A 'black hole' in the historical record due to the loss of almost all correspondence between 1669 and 1673 has concealed the presence of the Peningtons and Gulielma Springett in Tyler End Green for some two years before Gulielma's marriage to William Penn in April 1672. The discovery that there were several other Quaker families in the parish and that there were Quaker sympathies in the Squire's family as well as their mutually acknowledged kindred with William Penn, would seem to explain why Tyler End Green was a welcome haven for the Peningtons. A promising candidate for the house in which they lived has been identified.

Twentieth-century disputes - The insistence by the two 20th-century Vicars of Penn that the parish was William Penn's ancestral home created a surprising degree of contention. Mr Muspratt set out his case in considerable detail and almost all he said about William Penn's many interesting and varied links with the parish was true and indeed further supporting evidence has been revealed by this investigation. There is no doubt that the two families firmly believed they were related and it would be delightful to discover that they were, but to continue to insist on a genealogical link that has not been established is to fly in the face of the evidence and damage an otherwise good case.